Milwaukee Sports Trivia

Brewers, Bucks and Packers Fun
Facts and Challenges

200 questions to debate with your friends

Caleb Murphy

Introduction

Milwaukee has a rich history of sports dating back over a century. From the early baseball teams of the 1900s to today's Bucks, Brewers and Packers, the city's fans have enjoyed championship caliber teams and memorable athletes.

One of the first professional baseball teams to call Milwaukee home was the Brewers, who played in the minor leagues from 1886 to 1891. They helped spark early interest in the nation's pastime in the city. In the 1950s, the Braves brought Major League Baseball to Milwaukee and delighted fans with future Hall of Famers like Warren Spahn and Hank Aaron. Aaron would go on to hit his record-breaking 715th career home run as a Milwaukee Brave in 1974, cementing his legacy as one of the city's most beloved sports heroes.

While baseball has had an up and down presence in Milwaukee over the decades, pro football and basketball have provided more sustained success. The Packers dynasty of the 1960s delivered five NFL championships behind the legendary play of Vince Lombardi and stars like Bart Starr. Even after Lombardi's departure, Packers' traditions like the Lambeau Leap and Titletown moniker continue to this day. The Bucks joined the NBA in 1968 and gained popularity thanks to stars like Kareem Abdul-Jabbar and Ray Allen. They captured the 1971 NBA title, the city's only pro basketball championship to date.

Milwaukee's passionate fan support through many championship droughts is also part of its sports legacy. Miller Park and Fiserv Forum routinely sell out, proving Green Bay Packers fandom extends far beyond Wisconsin's borders. The city has also hosted major sporting events like the MLB All-Star Game in 2002 and the NCAA Final Four in 2004, showcasing its world-class sports facilities.

This book contains hundreds of trivia questions and fascinating facts to test your knowledge of these teams, players and memorable moments from over a century of Milwaukee sports history. Turn the page to start exploring all the stories, stats and championships that have made Milwaukee a celebrated destination for champions on the field and in the stands.

Milwaukee Sports Trivia

Question 1

Who holds the Milwaukee Brewers' record for most home runs in a single season?

Answer: Prince Fielder with 50 home runs in 2007. This achievement helped solidify Fielder as one of the premier power hitters in baseball during his career.

Question 2

In what year did the Milwaukee Bucks win their first NBA Championship?

Answer: 1971. Led by Kareem Abdul-Jabbar (then Lew Alcindor) and Oscar Robertson, the Bucks defeated the Baltimore Bullets in a four-game sweep to claim the title.

Question 3

Which Green Bay Packers player is famously known as "The Gunslinger"?

Answer: Brett Favre. Favre was known for his fearless and aggressive playing style, earning him this nickname during his prolific career with the Packers.

Question 4

What is the name of the stadium where the Milwaukee Brewers play their home games?

Answer: American Family Field (formerly Miller Park). The stadium, known for its fan-shaped retractable roof, opened in 2001 and provides a unique baseball experience regardless of weather conditions.

Question 5

Who was the MVP of the 2021 NBA Finals, leading the Milwaukee Bucks to victory?

Answer: Giannis Antetokounmpo. Giannis's dominant performance, including a 50-point game in the clinching Game 6, earned him Finals MVP honors and brought the Bucks their first championship in 50 years.

Question 6

Which Packers coach has the most Super Bowl victories?

Answer: Vince Lombardi, with victories in Super Bowls I and II. Lombardi's leadership and coaching philosophy left a lasting legacy in the NFL, and the Super Bowl trophy is named in his honor.

Question 7

Which Brewer won the National League MVP award in 2011?

Answer: Ryan Braun. Braun's exceptional season included a .332 batting average, 33 home runs, and 111 RBIs, which earned him the MVP award.

Question 8

Who was the Bucks' first draft pick in the 1969 NBA Draft?

Answer: Kareem Abdul-Jabbar (then known as Lew Alcindor). Kareem's arrival instantly transformed the Bucks into a competitive team, leading to their first NBA championship in 1971.

Question 9

How many NFL Championships (pre-Super Bowl era) have the Green Bay Packers won?

Answer: 11 championships. These titles, combined with their four Super Bowl victories, make the Packers one of the most successful franchises in NFL history.

Question 10

Who pitched the first no-hitter in Milwaukee Brewers history?

Answer: Juan Nieves in 1987. Nieves achieved this milestone against the Baltimore Orioles, marking a historic moment for the Brewers' franchise.

Question 11

In which year did the Milwaukee Bucks acquire Giannis Antetokounmpo in the NBA Draft?

Answer: 2013. Giannis, selected 15th overall, has since become one of the most dominant players in the league and a key figure in the Bucks' success.

Question 12

Which Packers quarterback led the team to victory in Super Bowl XLV?

Answer: Aaron Rodgers. Rodgers' performance in the 2010 season and Super Bowl XLV earned him Super Bowl MVP honors and cemented his status as one of the elite quarterbacks in the NFL.

Question 13

What year did the Milwaukee Brewers move from the American League to the National League?

Answer: 1998. This realignment allowed for new rivalries and brought the Brewers into the Central Division of the National League.

Question 14

Who is the all-time leading scorer for the Milwaukee Bucks?

Answer: Kareem Abdul-Jabbar. During his six seasons with the Bucks, Kareem scored a total of 14,211 points, a record that still stands today.

Question 15

Which Packers player is known for the "Lambeau Leap" celebration?

Answer: LeRoy Butler. Butler first performed the Lambeau Leap after a touchdown in 1993, creating a tradition that continues to this day.

Question 16

Who was the Brewers' manager when they reached the World Series in 1982?

Answer: Harvey Kuenn. Kuenn led the team to its only World Series appearance, where they lost to the St. Louis Cardinals in seven games.

Question 17

What was the original name of the Milwaukee Bucks' home arena, now known as the Fiserv Forum?

Answer: The MECCA (Milwaukee Exposition Convention Center Arena). The Bucks played at The MECCA from 1968 to 1988 before moving to the Bradley Center.

Question 18

Which Packers player holds the record for the most rushing yards in a single season?

Answer: Ahman Green, with 1,883 yards in 2003. Green's remarkable season remains the benchmark for Packers running backs.

Question 19

Who was the first Milwaukee Brewer inducted into the Baseball Hall of Fame?

Answer: Robin Yount. Yount, who played his entire career with the Brewers, was inducted in 1999 and is celebrated for his versatility and leadership.

Question 20

What year did the Milwaukee Bucks join the NBA?

Answer: 1968. The Bucks quickly found success, winning their first NBA championship just three years later in 1971.

Question 21

Which Packers linebacker was named MVP of Super Bowl XXXI?

Answer: Desmond Howard. Howard's 99-yard kickoff return for a touchdown was a key play in the Packers' victory over the New England Patriots.

Question 22

Who hit the famous "Walk-Off Grand Slam" for the Brewers in Game 1 of the 1982 ALCS?

Answer: Paul Molitor. Molitor's dramatic home run helped propel the Brewers to the World Series that year.

Question 23

Which Milwaukee Bucks player was known as the "Big Dog"?

Answer: Glenn Robinson. Robinson earned this nickname due to his scoring ability and impact on the court during his time with the Bucks.

Question 24

How many Super Bowl titles have the Green Bay Packers won?

Answer: Four (Super Bowls I, II, XXXI, and XLV). This success, combined with their pre-Super Bowl championships, underscores the Packers' rich history.

Question 25

Who is the Brewers' all-time leader in stolen bases?

Answer: Paul Molitor, with 412 stolen bases. Molitor's speed and base-running acumen made him one of the most dynamic players in Brewers history.

Question 26

Which Milwaukee Brewers player won the 2018 National League MVP award?

Answer: Christian Yelich. Yelich had an outstanding season, batting .326 with 36 home runs and 110 RBIs, leading the Brewers to the postseason.

Question 27

Who was the Milwaukee Bucks' first head coach?

Answer: Larry Costello. Costello coached the Bucks from their inaugural season in 1968 until 1976, leading them to their first NBA Championship in 1971.

Question 28

Which Green Bay Packers wide receiver caught the game-winning touchdown pass in Super Bowl XLV?

Answer: Greg Jennings. Jennings caught a 31-yard touchdown pass from Aaron Rodgers, contributing significantly to the Packers' victory over the Pittsburgh Steelers.

Question 29

What year did the Milwaukee Brewers franchise originally form, and under what name?

Answer: 1969, as the Seattle Pilots. The team moved to Milwaukee in 1970 and became the Brewers.

Question 30

Who is the Milwaukee Bucks' all-time leader in assists?

Answer: Paul Pressey. Pressey, known for his playmaking skills, recorded 3,272 assists during his time with the Bucks.

Question 31

Which Packers player is nicknamed "The Minister of Defense"?

Answer: Reggie White. White was a dominant defensive end and a key figure in the Packers' Super Bowl XXXI victory.

Question 32

Who is the Milwaukee Brewers' all-time leader in hits?

Answer: Robin Yount. Yount amassed 3,142 hits during his career with the Brewers, making him the franchise's all-time leader.

Question 33

What year did the Milwaukee Bucks draft Ray Allen?

Answer: 1996. Ray Allen was initially drafted by the Minnesota Timberwolves and then traded to the Bucks on draft night.

Question 34

Which Packers running back was named MVP of Super Bowl XXXII?

Answer: Terrell Davis. Note: This is a trick question. Terrell Davis was actually the MVP of Super Bowl XXXII, but he played for the Denver Broncos, not the Packers.

Question 35

Which Brewers pitcher won the 1981 American League Cy Young Award?

Answer: Rollie Fingers. Fingers had an exceptional season as a relief pitcher, helping the Brewers reach the postseason.

Question 36

Who is the Milwaukee Bucks' all-time leader in rebounds?

Answer: Kareem Abdul-Jabbar. Kareem grabbed 7,161 rebounds during his time with the Bucks.

Question 37

What year did the Green Bay Packers join the NFL?

Answer: 1921. The Packers are one of the oldest franchises in the NFL, with a storied history dating back to the early days of the league.

Question 38

Which Milwaukee Brewers player hit for the cycle in a 2018 game against the Cincinnati Reds?

Answer: Christian Yelich. Yelich hit for the cycle twice in the 2018 season, both times against the Reds.

Question 39

Who was the first Milwaukee Bucks player to win the NBA Rookie of the Year award?

Answer: Kareem Abdul-Jabbar (then Lew Alcindor) in 1970. His impressive debut season set the stage for a Hall of Fame career.

Question 40

Which Packers player holds the franchise record for the most interceptions in a career?

Answer: Bobby Dillon, with 52 interceptions. Dillon played for the Packers from 1952 to 1959.

Question 41

Who is the all-time leader in home runs for the Milwaukee Brewers?

Answer: Ryan Braun, with 352 home runs. Braun spent his entire career with the Brewers, becoming one of their most prolific hitters.

Question 42

What is the nickname given to the Milwaukee Bucks' defense during their 2021 championship run?

Answer: "The Wall." The Bucks' defense was known for its ability to contain opposing star players, particularly during their playoff series against the Brooklyn Nets.

Question 43

Which Packers player scored the winning touchdown in the "Ice Bowl"?

Answer: Bart Starr. Starr's quarterback sneak in the final seconds of the 1967 NFL Championship Game against the Dallas Cowboys secured a legendary victory for the Packers.

Question 44

Who was the first Milwaukee Brewer to win a Gold Glove Award?

Answer: George Scott. Scott won the Gold Glove as a first baseman in 1976, 1977, and 1978.

Question 45

Which Milwaukee Bucks player won the NBA's Sixth Man of the Year award in 2020?

Answer: Montrezl Harrell. Note: This is a trick question. Montrezl Harrell won the award, but he played for the Los Angeles Clippers, not the Bucks.

Question 46

What year did the Green Bay Packers win their first Super Bowl?

Answer: 1967, in Super Bowl I. The Packers defeated the Kansas City Chiefs 35-10.

Question 47

Who is the Milwaukee Brewers' all-time leader in RBIs?

Answer: Robin Yount, with 1,406 RBIs. Yount's consistent hitting and longevity helped him achieve this milestone.

Question 48

Which Milwaukee Bucks player was known for his iconic skyhook shot?

Answer: Kareem Abdul-Jabbar. The skyhook became Kareem's signature move and was nearly impossible to defend.

Question 49

Which Packers player holds the record for the most career sacks?

Answer: Clay Matthews, with 83.5 sacks. Matthews was a dominant force on the Packers' defense during his tenure with the team.

Question 50

Who was the first Milwaukee Brewer to have his number retired?

Answer: Hank Aaron. Although Aaron played only the final two seasons of his career with the Brewers, his impact on the game led the team to retire his number 44.

Question 51

Which Milwaukee Brewers pitcher was known for his distinctive handlebar mustache?

Answer: Rollie Fingers. Fingers' handlebar mustache became his trademark during his Hall of Fame career.

Question 52

Who was the Milwaukee Bucks' leading scorer during the 2020-2021 NBA season?

Answer: Giannis Antetokounmpo. Giannis averaged 28.1 points per game, leading the Bucks to their first championship in 50 years.

Question 53

Which Green Bay Packers player famously guaranteed a victory in Super Bowl III?

Answer: This is a trick question. Joe Namath guaranteed a victory in Super Bowl III, but he played for the New York Jets, not the Packers.

Question 54

What year did the Milwaukee Brewers first make the playoffs?

Answer: 1981. The Brewers made the playoffs as part of the American League East Division.

Question 55

Who is the Milwaukee Bucks' all-time leader in three-pointers made?

Answer: Ray Allen. Allen made 1,051 three-pointers during his time with the Bucks.

Question 56

Which Packers player was known for his "Lambeau Leap" after scoring touchdowns?

Answer: LeRoy Butler. Butler popularized the "Lambeau Leap" celebration in 1993.

Question 57

Who was the first Milwaukee Brewers player to win the Silver Slugger Award?

Answer: Cecil Cooper. Cooper won the Silver Slugger as a first baseman in 1980, 1981, and 1982.

Question 58

Which Milwaukee Bucks player won the NBA's Most Improved Player award in 2017?

Answer: Giannis Antetokounmpo. Giannis's significant improvement in his performance earned him the award.

Question 59

Which Packers player was known as "The Majik Man"?

Answer: Don Majkowski. Majkowski earned this nickname during his time as the Packers' quarterback in the late 1980s and early 1990s.

Question 60

Who is the Milwaukee Brewers' all-time leader in walks?

Answer: Robin Yount. Yount drew 966 walks during his career with the Brewers.

Question 61

What year did the Milwaukee Bucks trade for Oscar Robertson?

Answer: 1970. The acquisition of Robertson played a crucial role in the Bucks winning their first NBA championship in 1971.

Question 62

Which Packers player holds the record for the most consecutive starts?

Answer: Brett Favre. Favre started 297 consecutive games during his career, a record for a quarterback.

Question 63

Who was the first Milwaukee Brewer to hit 40 home runs in a single season?

Answer: Gorman Thomas. Thomas hit 45 home runs in 1979, becoming the first Brewer to reach this milestone.

Question 64

Who is the Milwaukee Bucks' all-time leader in steals?

Answer: Quinn Buckner. Buckner recorded 1,042 steals during his time with the Bucks.

Question 65

Which Packers player returned an interception for a touchdown in Super Bowl XLV?

Answer: Nick Collins. Collins' interception return for a touchdown was a pivotal moment in the Packers' victory over the Pittsburgh Steelers.

Question 66

Who was the Milwaukee Brewers' first manager?

Answer: Dave Bristol. Bristol managed the Brewers during their inaugural season in 1970.

Question 67

Which Milwaukee Bucks player was known as "The Big O"?

Answer: Oscar Robertson. Robertson was a key player in the Bucks' 1971 championship team.

Question 68

Who is the Green Bay Packers' all-time leader in receiving yards?

Answer: Donald Driver. Driver amassed 10,137 receiving yards during his career with the Packers.

Question 69

Which Brewers player won the National League batting title in 2018?

Answer: Christian Yelich. Yelich led the National League with a .326 batting average.

Question 70

What year did the Milwaukee Bucks retire Kareem Abdul-Jabbar's number 33?

Answer: 1993. Abdul-Jabbar's number was retired in recognition of his contributions to the team during his career.

Question 71

Who is the Green Bay Packers' all-time leader in passing yards?

Answer: Brett Favre. Favre threw for 61,655 yards during his career with the Packers.

Question 72

Which Brewers player was known for his powerful arm and playing right field?

Answer: Sixto Lezcano. Lezcano was known for his defensive skills and strong throwing arm during his time with the Brewers.

Question 73

Who was the first Milwaukee Bucks player to be named to the NBA All-Defensive Team?

Answer: Sidney Moncrief. Moncrief was known for his defensive prowess and was named to the All-Defensive Team five times.

Question 74

Which Packers coach led the team to victory in Super Bowl XLV?

Answer: Mike McCarthy. McCarthy's leadership helped guide the Packers to a 31-25 victory over the Pittsburgh Steelers.

Question 75

Who is the Milwaukee Brewers' all-time leader in strikeouts as a pitcher?

Answer: Ben Sheets. Sheets recorded 1,206 strikeouts during his career with the Brewers.

Question 76

Who was the first Milwaukee Bucks player to win the NBA MVP award?

Answer: Kareem Abdul-Jabbar. Abdul-Jabbar won the award in 1971, 1972, and 1974 during his time with the Bucks.

Question 77

Which Green Bay Packers player was known for his distinctive dance moves after scoring touchdowns?

Answer: Donald Driver. Driver's end zone celebrations were a fan favorite during his time with the Packers.

Question 78

Who is the Milwaukee Brewers' all-time leader in doubles?

Answer: Robin Yount. Yount hit 583 doubles during his career with the Brewers.

Question 79

What year did the Milwaukee Bucks hire Mike Budenholzer as head coach?

Answer: 2018. Budenholzer led the Bucks to their 2021 NBA Championship.

Question 80

Which Packers player holds the record for the longest punt return for a touchdown?

Answer: Desmond Howard. Howard returned a punt 92 yards for a touchdown during the 1996 season.

Question 81

Who is the only Milwaukee Brewer to win both MVP and Cy Young Awards?

Answer: Rollie Fingers. Fingers won both awards in 1981 as a relief pitcher.

Question 82

Which Milwaukee Bucks player was known as "The Greek Freak"?

Answer: Giannis Antetokounmpo. Giannis earned this nickname due to his exceptional athleticism and Greek heritage.

Question 83

Which Packers player has the most career rushing touchdowns?

Answer: Jim Taylor. Taylor scored 81 rushing touchdowns during his career with the Packers.

Question 84

What year did the Milwaukee Brewers move to Miller Park (now American Family Field)?

Answer: 2001. The move to the new stadium marked a new era for the Brewers franchise.

Question 85

Who was the first Milwaukee Bucks player to be named to the NBA All-Star Game?

Answer: Jon McGlocklin. McGlocklin was named an All-Star in 1969.

Question 86

Which Packers player is known for his record-setting 14-sack season in 1989?

Answer: Tim Harris. Harris' 14 sacks in 1989 remain a franchise record for a single season.

Question 87

Who is the Milwaukee Brewers' all-time leader in games played?

Answer: Robin Yount. Yount played in 2,856 games for the Brewers.

Question 88

Which Milwaukee Bucks player won the NBA Finals MVP in 2021?

Answer: Giannis Antetokounmpo. Giannis' dominant performance in the Finals earned him the MVP award.

Question 89

Which Packers player was known for the "Golden Boy" nickname?

Answer: Paul Hornung. Hornung earned this nickname due to his versatile play and blond hair.

Question 90

Who hit the game-winning home run for the Brewers in the 2018 NLDS Game 1?

Answer: Mike Moustakas. Moustakas' walk-off single in the 10th inning gave the Brewers a 3-2 win over the Colorado Rockies.

Question 91

Which Milwaukee Bucks player was known for his exceptional defense and won two Defensive Player of the Year awards?

Answer: Sidney Moncrief. Moncrief won the award in 1983 and 1984.

Question 92

Which Packers player holds the record for the most passing touchdowns in a single season?

Answer: Aaron Rodgers. Rodgers threw 48 touchdown passes during the 2020 season.

Question 93

Who was the first Milwaukee Brewers player to hit for the cycle?

Answer: Mike Hegan. Hegan hit for the cycle on September 3, 1976, against the Detroit Tigers.

Question 94

Which Milwaukee Bucks player was known for his shot-blocking ability and was named to the NBA All-Defensive First Team multiple times?

Answer: Kareem Abdul-Jabbar. Abdul-Jabbar was a dominant shot-blocker and defensive force during his career.

Question 95

Which Packers player holds the record for the most career receiving touchdowns?

Answer: Don Hutson. Hutson scored 99 receiving touchdowns during his career with the Packers.

Question 96

Who is the Milwaukee Brewers' all-time leader in saves?

Answer: Dan Plesac. Plesac recorded 133 saves during his career with the Brewers.

Question 97

Which Milwaukee Bucks player won the NBA Three-Point Contest in 2001?

Answer: Ray Allen. Allen's shooting prowess earned him the title during All-Star Weekend.

Question 98

Which Packers player was the first to rush for over 1,000 yards in a single season?

Answer: Tony Canadeo. Canadeo rushed for 1,052 yards during the 1949 season.

Question 99

What year did the Milwaukee Brewers win their first division title?

Answer: 1981. The Brewers won the American League East Division title that year.

Question 100

Which Milwaukee Bucks player set a franchise record for points in a single game with 57 points?

Answer: Michael Redd. Redd set the record on November 11, 2006, against the Utah Jazz.

Question 101

Who was the first Milwaukee Bucks player to be inducted into the Basketball Hall of Fame?

Answer: Kareem Abdul-Jabbar. Inducted in 1995, Abdul-Jabbar was a dominant force in the NBA, winning six MVP awards and six championships.

Question 102

Which Green Bay Packers coach has the most wins in franchise history?

Answer: Curly Lambeau. Lambeau, a co-founder of the Packers, coached the team from 1921 to 1949 and won 212 games.

Question 103

Who was the first Milwaukee Brewer to win the American League Rookie of the Year award?

Answer: Pat Listach. Listach won the award in 1992 after hitting .290 and stealing 54 bases.

Question 104

Which Milwaukee Bucks player scored the most points in a single season?

Answer: Kareem Abdul-Jabbar. Abdul-Jabbar scored 2,822 points during the 1971-72 season.

Question 105

Which Packers player was known for his "frozen tundra" quote about Lambeau Field?

Answer: John Facenda. The quote "the frozen tundra of Lambeau Field" was made famous by NFL Films narrator John Facenda, though not a player, it is often associated with the Packers.

Question 106

Who holds the record for the highest batting average in a single season for the Milwaukee Brewers?

Answer: Paul Molitor. Molitor batted .353 during the 1987 season.

Question 107

Which Milwaukee Bucks player was known as "Big Dog"?

Answer: Glenn Robinson. Robinson was a two-time NBA All-Star and played for the Bucks from 1994 to 2002.

Question 108

Who was the Green Bay Packers' starting quarterback before Brett Favre?

Answer: Don Majkowski. Known as "The Majik Man," Majkowski was the starter before Favre took over in 1992.

Question 109

Which Milwaukee Brewers player won the 2007 National League Rookie of the Year award?

Answer: Ryan Braun. Braun hit .324 with 34 home runs and 97 RBIs in his rookie season.

Question 110

Who is the Milwaukee Bucks' all-time leader in free throws made?

Answer: Sidney Moncrief. Moncrief made 3,505 free throws during his career with the Bucks.

Question 111

Which Packers player returned an interception 100 yards for a touchdown against the Rams in 2004?

Answer: Darren Sharper. Sharper's 100-yard interception return is one of the longest in Packers history.

Question 112

Who was the first Milwaukee Brewer to pitch a no-hitter?

Answer: Juan Nieves. Nieves pitched a no-hitter against the Baltimore Orioles on April 15, 1987.

Question 113

Which Milwaukee Bucks player holds the record for the most points scored in a playoff game?

Answer: Giannis Antetokounmpo. Giannis scored 50 points in Game 6 of the 2021 NBA Finals against the Phoenix Suns.

Question 114

Which Packers player was known as "The Gravedigger"?

Answer: Gilbert Brown. Brown earned the nickname for his dominant play as a defensive tackle and his celebratory move of pretending to shovel dirt.

Question 115

Who is the Milwaukee Brewers' all-time leader in stolen bases?

Answer: Paul Molitor. Molitor stole 412 bases during his career with the Brewers.

Question 116

Which Milwaukee Bucks player was known for his clutch shooting and was nicknamed "Mr. Clutch"?

Answer: Jon McGlocklin. McGlocklin was known for his reliable shooting in critical moments.

Question 117

Which Packers player holds the record for the most career tackles?

Answer: A.J. Hawk. Hawk recorded 1,118 tackles during his career with the Packers.

Question 118

Who hit the game-winning home run for the Brewers in Game 1 of the 1982 World Series?

Answer: Paul Molitor. Molitor had a five-hit game in the Brewers' 10-0 victory over the St. Louis Cardinals.

Question 119

Which Milwaukee Bucks player was known for his colorful hair and defensive skills?

Answer: Dennis Rodman. Although known more for his time with the Bulls and Pistons, Rodman briefly played for the Bucks and was always recognized for his distinctive look and defense.

Question 120

Which Packers player was known as "The Golden Boy"?

Answer: Paul Hornung. Hornung was a versatile player who won the Heisman Trophy in college and became a Hall of Famer in the NFL.

Question 121

Who was the first Milwaukee Brewer to lead the league in home runs?

Answer: Gorman Thomas. Thomas led the American League in home runs in 1979 and 1982.

Question 122

Which Milwaukee Bucks player was known as "The Big Dog"?

Answer: Glenn Robinson. Robinson earned this nickname for his dominant play and physical presence on the court.

Question 123

Which Packers player set a team record with 18 sacks in a single season?

Answer: Tim Harris. Harris set the record in 1989, showcasing his pass-rushing prowess.

Question 124

Who is the only Milwaukee Brewer to win a Gold Glove Award as a catcher?

Answer: Jonathan Lucroy. Lucroy won the Gold Glove in 2014 for his defensive excellence behind the plate.

Question 125

Which Milwaukee Bucks player was known for his skyhook shot?

Answer: Kareem Abdul-Jabbar. Abdul-Jabbar's skyhook became one of the most unstoppable moves in basketball history.

Question 126

Who is the all-time leading scorer for the Green Bay Packers?

Answer: Don Hutson. Hutson scored 825 points during his career, primarily as a wide receiver and kicker.

Question 127

Which Milwaukee Brewers player won the NL MVP award in 2018?

Answer: Christian Yelich. Yelich had an outstanding season, batting .326 with 36 home runs and 110 RBIs.

Question 128

Which Milwaukee Bucks player holds the record for the most assists in a single game?

Answer: Guy Rodgers. Rodgers dished out 24 assists in a game against the Detroit Pistons on December 21, 1968.

Question 129

Which Packers player is famous for his "Ice Bowl" quarterback sneak?

Answer: Bart Starr. Starr's game-winning sneak in the 1967 NFL Championship Game, known as the "Ice Bowl," is one of the most iconic plays in NFL history.

Question 130

Who was the first Milwaukee Brewers player to win the Gold Glove Award?

Answer: George Scott. Scott won the Gold Glove as a first baseman in 1972, 1973, and 1975.

Question 131

Which Milwaukee Bucks player was known for his long-range shooting and played during the team's inaugural season?

Answer: Jon McGlocklin. McGlocklin was one of the original Bucks and later became a long-time broadcaster for the team.

Question 132

Who was the Green Bay Packers' head coach before Vince Lombardi?

Answer: Ray McLean. McLean coached the Packers during the 1958 season before Lombardi took over in 1959.

Question 133

Which Brewers pitcher holds the record for the most strikeouts in a single game?

Answer: Ben Sheets. Sheets struck out 18 batters in a game against the Atlanta Braves on May 16, 2004.

Question 134

Which Milwaukee Bucks player set a franchise record for the most rebounds in a single game?

Answer: Swen Nater. Nater grabbed 33 rebounds in a game against the Atlanta Hawks on December 19, 1976.

Question 135

Which Packers player was known for his "Cheesehead" celebration?

Answer: Gilbert Brown. Brown would don a cheesehead hat after big plays, becoming a fan favorite for his antics.

Question 136

Who is the Milwaukee Brewers' all-time leader in home runs?

Answer: Ryan Braun. Braun hit 352 home runs during his career with the Brewers.

Question 137

Which Milwaukee Bucks player was nicknamed "The A-Train"?

Answer: Artis Gilmore. Gilmore played for the Bucks during the 1987-88 season and was known for his powerful presence in the paint.

Question 138

Which Packers player intercepted a record 11 passes in the 1943 season?

Answer: Irv Comp. Comp's 11 interceptions in 1943 stood as an NFL record for many years.

Question 139

Who was the first Milwaukee Brewers player to hit 50 home runs in a single season?

Answer: Prince Fielder. Fielder hit 50 home runs in 2007, becoming the youngest player at the time to reach that mark.

Question 140

Which Milwaukee Bucks player was known for his aggressive defense and was a key part of the "Fear the Deer" movement?

Answer: Jrue Holiday. Holiday's defensive prowess played a crucial role in the Bucks' 2021 championship run.

Question 141

Which Packers player holds the record for the most career interceptions?

Answer: Bobby Dillon. Dillon intercepted 52 passes during his career with the Packers from 1952 to 1959.

Question 142

Who was the first Milwaukee Brewer to win the Roberto Clemente Award?

Answer: Ryan Braun. Braun won the award in 2012, recognizing his contributions to the community.

Question 143

Which Milwaukee Bucks player was known as "The Professor" for his high basketball IQ?

Answer: Ersan Ilyasova. Ilyasova was known for his smart play and consistent shooting.

Question 144

Which Packers player was known as "The Minister of Defense"?

Answer: Reggie White. White was a dominant defensive end and a key player in the Packers' Super Bowl XXXI victory.

Question 145

Who is the Milwaukee Brewers' all-time leader in triples?

Answer: Paul Molitor. Molitor hit 98 triples during his career with the Brewers.

Question 146

Which Milwaukee Bucks player was known for his high-flying dunks and athleticism?

Answer: Marques Johnson. Johnson was a five-time All-Star known for his spectacular dunks and all-around play.

Question 147

Which Packers player set a record with 14 catches in a single playoff game?

Answer: Davante Adams. Adams caught 14 passes in a game against the Los Angeles Rams in the 2020 playoffs.

Question 148

Who was the first Milwaukee Brewer to win the American League MVP award?

Answer: Robin Yount. Yount won the MVP award in 1982 and again in 1989.

Question 149

Which Milwaukee Bucks player was known for his three-point shooting and was nicknamed "The Ray of Light"?

Answer: Ray Allen. Allen was one of the best shooters in NBA history and a key player for the Bucks during his time with the team.

Question 150

Which Packers player holds the record for the most passing yards in a single game?

Answer: Matt Flynn. Flynn threw for 480 yards in a game against the Detroit Lions on January 1, 2012.

Question 151

Who was the first head coach of the Milwaukee Bucks?

Answer: Larry Costello. Costello coached the Bucks from their inaugural season in 1968 until 1976, leading them to their first NBA championship in 1971.

Question 152

Which Packers player kicked the longest field goal in team history?

Answer: Mason Crosby. Crosby kicked a 58-yard field goal against the Detroit Lions on October 6, 2019.

Question 153

Who was the first Milwaukee Brewer to win a batting title?

Answer: Paul Molitor. Molitor won the batting title in 1987 with a .353 average.

Question 154

Which Milwaukee Bucks player was known for his ability to hit clutch shots and earned the nickname "Big Shot Bob"?

Answer: Robert Horry. Though known for his clutch shooting, Horry was never a Bucks player; he earned the nickname during his time with other NBA teams.

Question 155

Which Packers player holds the record for the most career rushing yards?

Answer: Ahman Green. Green rushed for 8,322 yards during his career with the Packers.

Question 156

Who hit the first home run in Milwaukee Brewers history?

Answer: Mike Hegan. Hegan hit the first home run for the Brewers on April 7, 1970, against the California Angels.

Question 157

Which Milwaukee Bucks player won the Sixth Man of the Year award in 2020?

Answer: No Milwaukee Bucks player won the Sixth Man of the Year award in 2020; the winner was Montrezl Harrell of the Los Angeles Clippers.

Question 158

Which Packers player was known for his acrobatic catches and played as a wide receiver from 1992 to 1999?

Answer: Robert Brooks. Brooks was known for his spectacular catches and playmaking ability.

Question 159

Who was the first Milwaukee Brewer to pitch in an All-Star Game?

Answer: Ken Sanders. Sanders pitched in the 1971 All-Star Game representing the Brewers.

Question 160

Which Milwaukee Bucks player set the record for most three-pointers made in a single season?

Answer: Ray Allen. Allen set the franchise record for most three-pointers made in a single season with 229 in the 2001-2002 season.

Question 161

Which Packers player holds the record for the most career sacks?

Answer: Clay Matthews III. Matthews recorded 83.5 sacks during his career with the Packers.

Question 162

Who was the first Milwaukee Brewer to be inducted into the Baseball Hall of Fame?

Answer: Robin Yount. Yount was inducted into the Hall of Fame in 1999 after a stellar career with the Brewers.

Question 163

Which Milwaukee Bucks player was known for his high-flying dunks and was part of the 2000 NBA Slam Dunk Contest?

Answer: Ray Allen. Allen participated in the 2000 Slam Dunk Contest, showcasing his athleticism.

Question 164

Which Packers player was known as "The Majik Man"?

Answer: Don Majkowski. Majkowski earned this nickname for his exciting play as the Packers' quarterback in the late 1980s.

Question 165

Who is the Milwaukee Brewers' all-time leader in runs batted in (RBIs)?

Answer: Robin Yount. Yount holds the record with 1,406 RBIs.

Question 166

Which Milwaukee Bucks player was nicknamed "The Alphabet"?

Answer: Giannis Antetokounmpo. Giannis earned this nickname due to the complexity of his last name.

Question 167

Which Packers player was known for his versatility and played multiple positions, including quarterback, halfback, and kicker?

Answer: Paul Hornung. Hornung's versatility made him one of the most valuable players in Packers history.

Question 168

Who threw the first no-hitter in Milwaukee Brewers history?

Answer: Juan Nieves. Nieves threw the no-hitter on April 15, 1987, against the Baltimore Orioles.

Question 169

Which Milwaukee Bucks player was known for his incredible shot-blocking ability and won the Defensive Player of the Year award in 2020?

Answer: Giannis Antetokounmpo. Giannis was recognized for his outstanding defensive play, earning the award in 2020.

Question 170

Which Packers player was known as "The Hammer"?

Answer: Fred Williamson. Though not a long-term Packer, Williamson earned this nickname for his hard-hitting style.

Question 171

Who was the first Milwaukee Brewer to hit three home runs in a single game?

Answer: Ted Kubiak. Kubiak hit three home runs in a game against the Boston Red Sox on July 18, 1970.

Question 172

Which Milwaukee Bucks player set a franchise record for points in a playoff game with 50 points?

Answer: Giannis Antetokounmpo. Giannis scored 50 points in Game 6 of the 2021 NBA Finals, leading the Bucks to their first championship in 50 years.

Question 173

Which Packers player holds the record for the most consecutive starts by a quarterback?

Answer: Brett Favre. Favre started 297 consecutive games for the Packers from 1992 to 2007.

Question 174

Who was the first Milwaukee Brewer to be named World Series MVP?

Answer: No Milwaukee Brewers player has been named World Series MVP, as the team has not yet won a World Series.

Question 175

Which Milwaukee Bucks player was known for his defensive prowess and won the NBA Defensive Player of the Year award in 1983 and 1984?

Answer: Sidney Moncrief. Moncrief's defensive skills earned him back-to-back Defensive Player of the Year awards.

Question 176

Who was the first Milwaukee Bucks player to win the NBA Rookie of the Year award?

Answer: Kareem Abdul-Jabbar. Then known as Lew Alcindor, he won the award in 1970 after averaging 28.8 points and 14.5 rebounds per game in his rookie season.

Question 177

Which Packers player has the most career touchdown receptions?

Answer: Don Hutson. Hutson, who played from 1935 to 1945, caught 99 touchdown passes, a record that stood for decades.

Question 178

Who was the first Milwaukee Brewer to win a Silver Slugger award?

Answer: Robin Yount. Yount won the Silver Slugger as a shortstop in 1980, recognizing him as one of the best offensive players at his position.

Question 179

Which Milwaukee Bucks player holds the franchise record for most steals in a single game?

Answer: Quinn Buckner. Buckner recorded 11 steals in a game against the Detroit Pistons on November 3, 1976.

Question 180

Which Packers player was known for his leap into the stands after scoring a touchdown, starting the "Lambeau Leap" tradition?

Answer: LeRoy Butler. Butler first performed the Lambeau Leap in 1993, and it has since become a beloved Packers tradition.

Question 181

Who was the first Milwaukee Brewer to hit for the cycle?

Answer: Mike Hegan. Hegan hit for the cycle on September 3, 1976, against the Detroit Tigers.

Question 182

Which Milwaukee Bucks player was known for his sharpshooting and won the NBA Three-Point Contest in 2001?

Answer: Ray Allen. Allen was one of the best shooters in NBA history and won the contest in 2001.

Question 183

Which Packers player holds the record for the most career points scored?

Answer: Mason Crosby. Crosby, a kicker, holds the record with over 1,700 points scored for the Packers.

Question 184

Who was the first Milwaukee Brewer to win the Cy Young Award?

Answer: Pete Vuckovich. Vuckovich won the award in 1982 after going 18-6 with a 3.34 ERA.

Question 185

Which Milwaukee Bucks player was known for his incredible athleticism and was nicknamed "Skywalker"?

Answer: Kenny Walker. Though better known for his time with the New York Knicks, Walker's nickname highlights his leaping ability.

Question 186

Which Packers player returned a fumble 77 yards for a touchdown in Super Bowl XXXI?

Answer: Desmond Howard. Howard's fumble return was a key play in the Packers' victory over the New England Patriots.

Question 187

Who is the Milwaukee Brewers' all-time leader in hits?

Answer: Robin Yount. Yount recorded 3,142 hits during his career with the Brewers.

Question 188

Which Milwaukee Bucks player was known for his dominant shot-blocking and was nicknamed "The Secretary of Defense"?

Answer: Bob Lanier. Lanier played for the Bucks in the 1980s and was known for his strong defensive presence.

Question 189

Which Packers player holds the record for the most rushing touchdowns in a single season?

Answer: Ahman Green. Green scored 15 rushing touchdowns in the 2003 season.

Question 190

Who was the first Milwaukee Brewer to win a Gold Glove Award at shortstop?

Answer: Robin Yount. Yount won the Gold Glove in 1982 for his stellar defensive play.

Question 191

Which Milwaukee Bucks player was known for his high-flying dunks and won the NBA Slam Dunk Contest in 2022?

Answer: No Milwaukee Bucks player won the Slam Dunk Contest in 2022; the winner was Obi Toppin of the New York Knicks.

Question 192

Which Packers player holds the record for the most career fumble recoveries?

Answer: Brett Favre. Favre recovered 27 fumbles during his career, a testament to his longevity and hustle on the field.

Question 193

Who was the first Milwaukee Brewer to be named an All-Star?

Answer: Don Money. Money was selected as an All-Star in 1974, representing the Brewers at second base.

Question 194

Which Milwaukee Bucks player was known for his versatility and played both guard and forward positions during his career?

Answer: Michael Redd. Redd was a versatile scorer and played multiple positions during his time with the Bucks.

Question 195

Which Packers player was the first to have his number retired?

Answer: Don Hutson. Hutson's number 14 was retired by the Packers in 1951 in honor of his legendary career.

Question 196

Who was the first Milwaukee Brewer to lead the league in home runs?

Answer: Gorman Thomas. Thomas led the American League in home runs in 1979 with 45 homers.

Question 197

Which Milwaukee Bucks player set a franchise record for points in a single game with 57 points?

Answer: Michael Redd. Redd scored 57 points against the Utah Jazz on November 11, 2006.

Question 198

Which Packers player holds the record for the most career interceptions returned for touchdowns?

Answer: Herb Adderley. Adderley returned seven interceptions for touchdowns during his career with the Packers.

Question 199

Who was the first Milwaukee Brewer to win the ALCS MVP award?

Answer: No Milwaukee Brewers player has won the ALCS MVP award, as the team has not advanced to the World Series as the American League champion since the format's inception.

Question 200

Which Milwaukee Bucks player was known for his defensive skills and was a four-time All-Defensive Team selection?

Answer: Paul Pressey. Pressey was a key defensive player for the Bucks in the 1980s and a pioneer in the "point forward" role.

Made in the USA
Monee, IL
29 October 2024

68800750R00039